l boy still has his gun aimed on Lawrence. Lawrence has his hands raised above him still. Lawrence gestures

earby, whereas to me it seems a poor place, some men find it marvellous. Tomorrow m   ow the T

aster, wailing and firing gunshots too. One of them plucks a red flag from the ground   759.2   . The ga

awrence and starts speaking, "This thing that you work against Aqaba, what profit do   ART   it?" As

ght in the eyes, then he turns to the crowd shouting, "I am Auda, does Auda serve?" The invisible crowd cha

turns back to Lawrence and Ali and sits down again. A man sitting behind Ali speaks now he cajoles, "And

ba... for money..." Auda interrupts, "No!" Lawrence continues, "... for Faisal." Again he butts in "No!" "... M

l by the dark interior of the tent, a group of shadowy figures sits in the foreground, watching the procession.

nd mountains trail away into the distance, a few thin clouds hang in the sky above them. The scene is comple

ment, framed by the deep purple sky, the mountain peaks jutting up into it behind him. Then Lawrence dash

n ancient wound!" Lawrence is incensed, he doesn't get it. He swings round again, not knowing which way t

e's eyes widen in shock. Horror passes across his face, the purple sky framing his head. He whispers the man

the Nefud." Auda calls after him, "It was written then?" Then he adds under his breath, "Better to have left h

somewhere else. Two soldiers stand guard on the top of the tower. They ring the alarm as the army comes th

ung to the ground, the hind legs of the horse land on his stomach, splattering his guts across the sand. The ho

in the distance. It's impossible to make out whether it's the sound of the massive waves breaking, or artillery

t seem to understand Ali's words, "I am none of those things Ali, "What then?" "Don't know." He looks dow

He swings round and heads for the exit, Ali follows. He keeps glancing across at him disbelievingly. He repe

his camel below. He bares his loaded fists at him and yells, "Paper...! Paper...!" The notes flutter down throu

nswers arrogantly, "Why not, Moses did!" He gallops off leaving Auda, contemptuous, bellowing into the n

norrow the finest sheets, in the finest room, in the finest hotel in Cairo." This does little to encourage the boy

l sand and dust. The huge feet of the camel plod relentlessly across the foreground. The landscape passes but

ange sky dissolves into pale blue mountains which stretch across the background. The riders are being pound

s if the camels front legs have given way, but then it starts to sink into the sand. The more he tries to walk, th

inal leap forwards and slams down on him with all his weight. Ramish and Lawrence are perfectly still for a

ead, buries it in the sand and cries. The two of them just lie there, belly down, faces in the sand. The harsh w

nvisible, their faces and robes covered with dirt and sand as they plod through the misty landscape. Barbed w

ehind it. He's running through the building yelling "Lawrence! Lawrence!" But still Lawrence doesn't respo

The deep sound of its horn echoes over the dunes, as scrub blusters around in the foreground. The two of the

nd still midway between their shoulders. The man on the bike has one foot on the ground, as he yells over to

ourtyard. Lawrence leads him by the arm and they head up the steps into the building. The soldier calls after

asting an eye at the boy, "You can't take him in there, sir!" But Lawrence pretends not to hear him. The sold

ompously, "Lawrence, are you off your head?!" Lawrence replies calmly, "No, oddly enough I'm not!" The

Turks have gone?" Lawrence still doesn't look at him as he says, "No, they're still there, but they have no bo

o one responds. He steps back slightly and says, "You'd better talk to Allenby!" Lawrence sounds surprised "

t they are being stared at by all the other men. Brighton stands on the other side of the boy as they make their

ts behind a large oak desk, his hands clasped in front of him on the desk. He is moustached, wearing a milita

s, "True." "... and it will be further behind your right when you go for Jerusalem." The General muses, "Am

, then Lawrence says pointedly, "Yes, I know!" The General sits back, after another pause he says abruptly, "

l... it!" The General slowly drops his eyes to the desk in front of him, then gets up, and walks towards the tw

righton, before he can ask him for his opinion Lawrence butts in contemptuously "I know what he thinks!" T

wn the stairs. He waves his stick in front of him in such a way as to indicate strategy, his voice fading in and

he pauses and casts Lawrence a glance, "... Major Lawrence..." Fans whirr behind their heads. The General

l sits down, "Hummm... Well if we can see it, so can the Turk. If he's using four divisions to fend off a handf

ixed on the General, "... Have we?" The General shirks the question, looks across at the other men leaning ba

s on listing his demands "... More money." The General sucks on his cigarette and asks without looking ove

and stares back at the crowd of officers who stare across at him. They are crowded round the mess door. Law

He asks without lifting his eyes from the ground, "Are you really going to give them artillery, sir?" Brighton

r a moment and pauses for breath. As an old man approaches from the other direction, he stops and asks him

ous cameras and places them on the floor beside him. Faisal   places a

isal replies patiently, "That is so." Bently adds, provocat   alwa

vill have some facts and figures put on paper for you... Y   urki

harshly than I hope you can imagine." Bently stares dir   r. B

y looks directly back at Fiasal, "It's very simple sir. I'm   slightly,

he rails and onto the sand, coach by coach. Bentley lurk   is o

e, now standing directly in the line of fire, fires off anoth

the boy with a nod of his head saying, "Call off your men!" Auda gestures to the boy to put his gun down ar
ks to buy you, friends of Faisal!" He points a long, dark finger in the direction of Lawrence. He mounts his h
ping hooves are like thunder. Auda and the Harif army descend the hill in a cloud of dust and sand. The How
erif Ali answers, Lawrence glances round to look at him, "We do it for Faisal of Mecca. The Harif do not wo
back in unison "No... No..!" Then still not satisfied, he emerges from the tent and addresses the crowd direct
w it seems Auda has got old, and lost his taste for fighting!" Auda's words are vexed, "It is as well that you s
to drive away the Turks..." Lawrence leans over, his profile is very close to Auda's face now, as finally, and
e army curves endlessly around the side of a rock, forming a huge arc across the sands. Three men waving th
y silent. Then there is the sound of approaching footsteps on the shale. Ali and Lawrence clamber to the top
down towards the camp. Men form a circle round a man, who lies motionless, sprawled across the sand, his
urn and says furiously to himself, "I didn't come here to watch a tribal blood bath!" Then he runs over to Aue
name, "Gasim!" Gasim stares up at him petrified, his arms strapped behind his back. Sweat pours down his fa
!" Ali paces alongside Lawrence, who stares concentratedly down at the ground. "There is no shame Lawrer
dering into view. As they appear round the corner, they are only visible through the cloud of smoke. Then the
plunges on indifferently, his rump gleaming with sweat. He thunders off into a haze of dirt and gunfire. Sold
unding through the night. The headland which curves around the bay turns pale mauve as the sun goes down
t the flowers dripping in his hand, the waves crashing behind him. He looks towards the city, "God I love thi
s "Sinaii?" He turns to Lawrence's servants, "With these?" Lawrence heads off but then turns back on Ali ane
the air. He descends, and staring at Lawrence, says through clenched teeth, "There is no gold at Aqaba... No
t, "Moses was a prophet!... and beloved of God!" Ali moves into the foreground, his eyes gleaming in the da
vho slump exhaustedly on their camels, heads drooped as they motion forwards. The sky gradually fades to p
doesn't change. Lawrence's compass drops, from the height of the camel onto the sand. He doesn't seem to r
by the wind. Sand blows across the foreground, across the background, into their faces and eyes. One by one
quicker he sinks. His camel balks at the soft sand. It struggles for a moment and then pulls itself up again, an
cond. They both kneel and look over in the direction of Daoud. Lawrence steadies Ramesh, his hands on his
ds bluster over them, there, in the middle of the desert. Then after what seems like an eternity Lawrence look
e criss crosses the foreground. They seem not to notice it. The camels just carry on riding at the same pace. T
. He's barely recognisable behind the mask of sand and dirt caking his face. His eyes are cast down to the gr
remain perfectly still as they watch the boat pass, the door still bashing against its frame behind them. Then
em on the other side, "Who are you?" His voice is almost drowned in the wind. It reaches Lawrence as a ver
wrence, he's confused too, "Are you taking him in there sir?" Lawrence looks back over his shoulder and an
stares after Lawrence as he walks into the bar, eyes on his stained robes as he says pompously, to himself, "
her officer standing to Lawrence's left says, "Go on Lawrence, clear off won't you!" Another cry comes fron
! Prisoners sir, we took them prisoner sir, the entire garrison." His fist shakes as it clasps the glass. He sudde
eneral Allenby?!" "Yes, he's in command now. Murray's gone." Lawrence stares down at the bar, "Well that
ay through the crowd. Lawrence turns to him, "I suppose I'd better shave!" Brighton looks back, smiling. He
jacket adorned with stripes. He looks across at Lawrence, and continues "... You're an interesting man, Law
going for Jerusalem!" Lawrence answers him plainly, with absolute confidence, "Yes." The General's disdain
m promoting you Major!" Lawrence is not remotely inspired, "I don't think that's a very good idea, sir." "I d
other men saying, as if to himself, in a tone of self-enforced disbelief, "Rubbish! Rubbish!" Then he turns fu
en unexpectedly Brighton springs to his feet and bursts out emotionally, "I think he should be recommended
t. "Look here now, If I'm to Jerusalem, I must concentrate, not dissipate." Lawrence says something back to
ints over to the glass doors which extend the whole length of the room, "... Shall we go outside?" The entou
of bandits he'll withdraw!" "He daren't withdraw, Arabia's part of his empire. If he withdraws, he'll never g
on his chair says, "Have we any ambitions in Arabia, Brighton?" Brighton is also non-committal. His voice
t him, "How much more?" Lawrence is definitive, "Twenty-five thousand now..." He ponders, "... a lot more
nce gathers up his robe and slowly, uncertainly walks over to the opening. The group of men pull back a little
ips in, "I was wondering that, sir. It might be deuce difficult to get it back again!" Dryden adds cautiously, "
"Excuse me friend, who do these bags belong to?" The old man answers without turning his head "To Prince
nall clock on the table in front of him. He turns to Bentley and says expectantly "Now...", and Bentley starts.
s, calm. "It restricts us to small things." Bentley adds, "It's intended to!" Faisal asks, "Do you know General
railways!" "I do sir. Major Lawrence is in charge of all this, is he?" Faisal explains "My army is made up o
tley, are taken care of until the British can relieve us of them, according to the code... I should like you to no
nd half smiling replies, "Indeed? You do not seem a romantic man." "Oh no, but certain influential men back
he horrendous event. Smoke streams across the desert towards the army, which waits over the next dune. The
heeded. Slowly the firing clatters to a halt. He turns around and with a tremendous sweep of his right arm, hi

The boy rides off. "This honours the unworthy... I've only just begun to teach him." "... And what are you te

ys, "Dine with me English... Dine with the Howeitat Harif." He looks across the whole camp and bellows, "

pelts across the sands to greet them. They charge past the group then they arc round, and finally encircle then

t." Auda concedes, but arrogantly, "Well if it is in a man to be a servant Sherif Ali, he could find worse maste

uda, does Auda serve?" The crowd yells "No", again in unison. Rounds of bullets crack through the sky. He t

tent, you fool!" Ali says, "And yet this is a fool that the Turks cannot buy!" Auda turns to Lawrence, "I will t

onfidence, he adds, "He will come because it is his pleasure!" Auda's expression is masked by a dark shadov

silhouetted against the blue sky. As the army leaves the camp behind, a faint shrill sound fills the air. As they

hill. They make for a ridge. Ali stretches his finger out in front of him. They look across at a sandy landsca

gs splayed. Blood oozes from his chest. The men shuffle forwards, getting closer and closer to the man, yet

e crooks his gun. He looks at Lawrence, and seeing his expression says, "It is the law Lawrence." "The law s

e same man that Lawrence saved from a certain death in the Nefud Desert! Lawrence asks him slowly, "Did

necessary... You saved his life, then you took it. The writing is still yours." Lawrence looks up at him, shakir

ns the haze and storms into view. One of the guards dashes for his gun. He rests it on the wall of the turret ar

g behind a barricade fire at horses as they rush at them. Two horses are hit, their front legs crumpling under t

going down right there, you see it. A camel lopes along the beach silhouetted in the distance, against the silve

At that moment the dull sound of an explosion shatters everything. Both men glance across to the town. A fir

onto the leather strap which harnesses his pistol, says, "Look Ali if any of your Bedouin were to arrive in Ca

is yelling now, "No great ox!" Lawrence stares cautiously back at him, then says with a barefaced confidenc

res out after Lawrence. Auda leans over to him and says, "He said there was gold here. He lied... He is not po

e terrain is hard and cracked. It seems like an endless expanse, interrupted only by massive rocks that jab vi

olods on. As the camel behind steps forwards, it kicks some sand over it, making it virtually invisible. Gradua

scarves around their mouths. The camels shy away from the wind, but are yanked forwards by the riders. La

of it. Daoud's left, treading the sand like a drowning man. The more he struggles, the further he sinks. He's u

Only Daoud's terrified face is visible now, poking out of the sand, as he desperately strains his neck to keep i

t the spot where Daoud finally sank. A small trickle of sand still pours into the centre of the hole, gradually fi

ns part of a dilapidated fence, which flanks a dusty pathway, leading to a ruined building. Gradually the falle

oor swings relentlessly in the background. Lawrences dazed face lurches into the foreground. Ramesh chuck

ver to the top of the nearby dune and look across. They help each other to steady as they stare out through th

He stares out through the foreground, his expression unchanging. He sees the man, he hears the man, but he

." The soldier steps back a few paces to look up at the building. Lawrence and the boy walk through a shady

he thinks he look like!" The bar's crowded with men in uniform, the hubbub of their voices reverberating rou

ound, "Yes, come on Lawrence, clear off!" The officer standing next to him raises his arm at the boy and say

nnerved, seems to be losing it. He continues with a slight shake in his voice, "Well that's not entirely true, we

he right direction." His voice sounds wobbly again, "First I want a room, with a bed, with sheets." Brighton

n at Lawrence's dusty garb and replies amusedly, "Yes, and we'd better find you some trousers too!" This spa

closes the file which is laid out on the table in front of him and leans further forwards, "You're an interesting

he doesn't enjoy agreeing with Lawrence. "Very well, Aqaba behind my right!" Lawrence's words are empha

u. I want you to go back and... carry on the good work." Lawrence replies in hushed tones, "No... Thank you

awrence and bellows, "What do you mean coming here dressed like that... amateur theatricals!" Lawrence lo

tion sir!" He pauses a moment and adds, "... I don't think it matters what his motives were." He thinks on for

s not audible. As they descend officers lean over a balcony and gaze down at them. Again the General can be

him dutifully. "So you held down the Turkish Desert army... with a thousand Arabs?!" Lawrence puts his ha

gain." Brighton leans forward and speaks, "I wonder who will?" Lawrence, still standing, replies certainly, ".

"Difficult suggestion, sir." Lawrence is incredibly emphatic. "I want to know sir. If I can tell them in your na

General glances across at the men, still sitting in front of the fountain and raises a questioning eyebrow at

om for Lawrence. They seem fascinated by him, unable to take their eyes off him. Lawrence walks a little w

rtillery and you've made them independent." The General holds his stick behind his back as he walks, his an

e man wearing the white hat speaks again. He has an American accent, "You're not Prince Faisal by any cha

n I find Major Lawrence?" Faisal returns the question "Is that what you've come for?" Bentley smiles slightl

Bentley looks up and says, "Watch out for Allenby. He's a slim customer." Faisal leans forwards a little, as if

tribes are led by the tribal leaders." Bentley interrupts, "Well your people do think very highly of Major La

n he gestures towards Bentley's notepad. Bentley replies "Yes sir... Is that the influence of Major Lawrence?"

ve that the time has come for America to lend her weight to the patriotic struggle against Germany... er, and

g indiscriminately at the fallen coaches. Bullets pelt into the side of the train and ricochet off the rails. The s

ing behind it, he yells the crowd to come on. One by one the soldiers of the army begin to yell, each raising l

Published on the occasion of *Words from the Arts Council Collection*, an Arts Council Collection exhibition toured by National Touring Exhibitions from the Hayward Gallery, London, for the Arts Council of England.

Exhibition tour:

City Museum and Art Gallery, Plymouth	4 May – 20 July 2002
Arts Centre, Aberystwyth	21 September – 10 November
City Art Gallery, York	16 November 2002 – 5 January 2003
Gallery Oldham	8 March – 27 April
The City Gallery, Leicester	3 May – 22 June

Exhibition selected by Fiona Bradley, Isobel Johnstone and Martin Thomas
Exhibition organized by Sophie Allen, Emma Mahony and Frances Munk

Catalogue designed by UNA (London) designers
Printed in England by The Beacon Press

Cover and endpapers: Fiona Banner, *The desert*, 1994-95 (cat. 5)(details)

Published by Hayward Gallery Publishing, London SE1 8XX, UK
© Hayward Gallery 2002
Artworks © the artists 2002 (unless stated otherwise)
Photographs: Mike Fear (unless stated otherwise)

ISBN 1 85332 226 1

Hayward Gallery Publishing titles are distributed outside North and South America and Canada by Cornerhouse Publications, 70 Oxford Street, Manchester M1 5NH (tel. 0161 200 1503; fax. 0161 200 1504; email: publications@cornerhouse.org; http://www.cornerhouse.org/publications).

For further information about works in the Arts Council Collection, please write to Isobel Johnstone, Curator of the Arts Council Collection, Hayward Gallery, SBC, Royal Festival Hall, London SE1 8XX.

words from the Arts Council Collection

The contemporary world is alive with verbal communication, the linguistic gymnastics of the media, commerce and politics, and the prevalent psychological strategies for counselling and consultation. Email and the Internet are stretching English language versatility globally. Artists have long been aware of ways in which words can give power to their art, and it is not surprising that many contemporary British artists are continuing to use language as the medium for very distinctive visual forms of expression.

There was much to choose from in selecting this exhibition, even within the time-span of the Collection, which has 3,000 original sculptures and paintings among a total of 7,000 works, including photographs, artists' prints, multiples and videos. Our aim initially was to focus on new work but it proved difficult to deny earlier work a significant place. Important paintings by Ben Nicholson and David Hockney, for example, reflect Cubist and Expressionist ideas, and fine examples of pure text by British artists of the 1970s demonstrate the serious intent of giving new accessibility, breadth and clarity to a 'visual art' experience.

In 1979, the Arts Council toured a Collection exhibition called *Languages*, selected by Rudi Fuchs who, then Director of Eindhoven Museum, is now Director of the Stedelijk Museum in Amsterdam. It was cutting-edge and quite esoteric for its time. Here we have set out to make a wider selection, one that is still challenging and also engaging.

Isobel Johnstone
Curator, Arts Council Collection, Hayward Gallery

Martin Thomas
Exhibitions Officer, Plymouth City Museum and Art Gallery

The Hayward Gallery, as custodian of the Arts Council Collection, the nation's primary loan collection of modern and contemporary British art, immensely values partnerships in the creation of exhibitions selected from works within it. Such collaborations make it possible to present the Collection in a new light and to make sure that it is accessible to a wide audience. We have particularly enjoyed working with Plymouth City Museum and Art Gallery on the development of *Words*, and are delighted to launch the tour of this new exhibition there. I should especially like to thank Martin Thomas, Exhibitions Officer, for helping to select the exhibition and writing about the process, and Sarah Norrish, for her work with Helen Luckett, the Hayward Gallery's Education Programmer, on a lively outreach programme.

Fiona Bradley, Exhibitions Curator at the Hayward Gallery, has written a lucid introduction that reveals strategies and illuminates the effects and meaning of the works in the exhibition. I thank her heartily for this valuable contribution to a subject that has clearly much life in it yet. We are indebted to Nick Bell and Silke Klinnert for their design of the catalogue. Catalogue production has been led most ably as ever by our Art Publisher, Linda Schofield, and our Publishing Co-ordinator, Caroline Wetherilt. The exhibition has been organized by Sophie Allen and Emma Mahony, Exhibition Organizers at the Hayward Gallery. My thanks go to them, and to the Collection team: Isobel Johnstone, Jill Constantine, Isabel Finch, Frances Munk and Richard Nesham, as well as to the Hayward Gallery's technical crew, in particular Steve Bullas, who will lead the installation team throughout the tour.

Finally, but by no means least, I should like to thank all those artists whose inventions have the power to arouse such curiosity and give such pleasure.

Susan Ferleger Brades
Director, Hayward Gallery

The written, painted, collaged and spoken word has played
a particularly important part in the development of art in the
twentieth and now the twenty-first centuries. As language has floated
ever freer from the restraints imposed by convention, advances in
literary theory, literature and poetry have allowed words to slide
away from accustomed usage to form new alliances; to be emptied
of old meaning and refreshed with new. Art has responded to this
process, and has on occasion been a driving force within it. Many of
the movements through which twentieth-century art history has been
mapped have included writers as well as artists – Cubism, Futurism,
Dada and Surrealism all used words as well as images as vehicles
for their particular form of artistic revolt, while, later in the century,
Conceptual Art elevated verbal description, definition and instruction
to an art form in its own right, habitually choosing words instead of
images as the most appropriate expression of an idea.

Artists working today make increasingly inventive use of language,
their discoveries often rooted in the researches of the past. They
insert words into the visual field where we might and where we
might not expect them. These words sometimes take the form of a
caption – a title or verbal punch line to a visual joke. They
sometimes work as collage in the tradition of the Cubists, the found
languages of newsprint or graffiti sharing space with more artistically
invented figurative or abstract imagery. They sometimes replace
such imagery altogether, operating as coded stand-ins for absent
visual references, or usurping the position of such references so that
the language we see is the art we must understand.

Glenn Baxter uses the language – both written and drawn – of
jokes and cartoons. Taking the form of captioned line drawings,
drawing and caption borrowing heavily from recognizable genres,
his work tells a joke at art's expense. Both of the artist's works in
this exhibition use in their captions the kind of pseudo-intellectual
modern art lover's jargon perceived to be used among the self-
styled *cognoscenti* and pilloried in the popular press. With his *"I find
his attempts to clarify the neo-plasticist stance a trifle wearing" muttered
Ken*, 1978 (cat. 6) and *"To me the window is still a symbolically loaded
motif" drawled Cody*, 1981 (cat. 7) Baxter uses words to point out the
potential meaninglessness of language once it has been over-used,
while at the same time hinting that there may well be less to 'modern
art' than meets the eye.

GLEN BAXTER | 6
"*I find his attempts to clarify the
neo-plasticist stance a trifle
wearing*" muttered Ken, 1978

" I FIND HIS ATTEMPTS TO CLARIFY
THE NEO-PLASTICIST STANCE A
TRIFLE WEARING" MUTTERED KEN

"To me the window is still a symbolically loaded motif" drawled Cody, 1981

"TO ME THE WINDOW IS STILL
, A SYMBOLICALLY LOADED MOTIF"
DRAWLED CODY

Glen Baxter 1981

David Shrigley's fragile drawings and faltering, handwritten captions are more subtle. Using the visual vocabulary of the cartoon or visual joke, they set up propositions in the mind and memory of the viewer, opening a space either for recognition and empathy or alienation and mockery. The artist seems not to know whether we will understand him or think he is completely mad – his strange visions, although they make a simultaneously visual and verbal appeal, are curiously self-sufficient: 'See the little creature in the giant cage rattling about like a pea in a drum. We are similar, I think, it and I (until my parents return from their holiday in Cyprus)' (cat. 31). In this drawing, the vast intricacies of the creature's cage match the impenetrability of the artist's thought, which he seeks nevertheless to transmit to us as directly as possible, mistakes and all.

Both Baxter and Shrigley use language to support the meaning of the visual element of their work, drawing on a recognizable convention through which to do so. Michael Craig-Martin's *Kid's Stuff 1-7*, 1973 (cat. 10) works in a similar way, although the convention he uses is that of the title of an artwork rather than the punch line of a joke. Hand writing captions within the frame of each of the seven images that make up the work, the artist uses language consciously to direct the viewer's experience and understanding of it. The work consists of seven small mirrors, positioned so that as the viewer approaches each one, the dominant image is that of his or her own reflection. The artist, speaking in the first person, dictates the meaning of each successive reflection – 'How strange it is to be my present age'; 'I feel I know myself'; 'I recall how it was being half my present age'; 'Did I feel I knew myself?'; 'I remember wondering how it would be to be twice my age'; 'It is not how I imagined'; 'How strange it would be to be twice my present age'. As past, present, future and conditional tenses merge, so too do the personae of artist and viewer – Craig-Martin's first person narrative inevitably becomes our own.

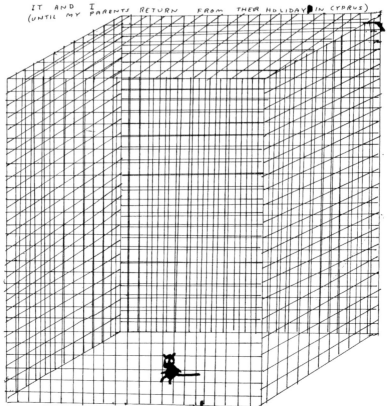

SEE THE LITTLE ▪ CREATURE IN THE GIANT CAGE
RATTLING ABOUT LIKE A PEA IN A DRUM
WE ARE SIMILAR , I THINK
IT AND I
(UNTIL MY PARENTS RETURN FROM THEIR HOLIDAY IN CYPRUS)

I feel I know myself.

How strange it is to be
my present age.

John Hilliard's *Cause of Death*, 1974 (cat. 22), also from the 1970s and a classic example of the Conceptual Art of that period, uses language similarly to direct the meaning of the image, and to point out to the viewer that both visual and verbal information is not necessarily always to be trusted. The artist presents four images of the same apparently dead body lying on the ground outside. Each image looks complete in itself, but, taken as one of four, is clearly only a fragment of a larger original, which has been cropped four ways. Each crop presents an entirely different narrative scenario of which the dead body is the result. Mimicking the way in which the police might present scene-of-the-crime photographic evidence, the artist gives the viewer a choice, captioning the four alternatives as he goes. First, the figure, lying surrounded by rocks, has been 'crushed'. Then, we are shown water nearby, and are asked to consider another possibility – 'drowned'. Next, a fire is revealed – 'burned'. Finally, a bridge – maybe the figure 'fell'. We never see the entire image, nor are the captions ever made to work against each other. Rather, the conflicting meanings of both kinds of information are held in a dramatic tension, which repeatedly resists resolution.

The second half of the twentieth century saw the rise of film and video as accepted media for gallery-based art, and as challenging vehicles for artists' thoughts and ideas. Moving images may come with audible sound or the silent voice-over of the written or printed caption can be developed into a fully-integrated soundtrack. Willie Doherty's *At the End of the Day*, 1994 (cat. 12) is a video projection made in Derry in the weeks following the announcement of the cease-fire in Northern Ireland. The film shows a country road at dusk or dawn, with the camera in the front seat of a car driving slowly towards an improvised roadblock. The car pulls up at the roadblock, waits awhile, and then we hear a voice – 'Let's not lose sight of the road ahead'. The voice is that of an Irishman. Once he has spoken, the film appears to loop back, and the car begins its journey again, arriving once more at the roadblock – 'There's no future in the past'. As the car repeats its trip, the voice runs through a series of phrases – 'At the end of the day it's a new beginning'; 'Let's not repeat the mistakes of the past'; 'At the end of the day there's no going back'; 'We're all in this together'; 'The only way is forward'; 'We have to forget the past and look to the future'; 'We're entering a new phase'; 'Nothing can last forever' – before beginning again with 'Let's not lose sight of the road ahead'. Each phrase speaks the meaningless language of the cliché embedded in the

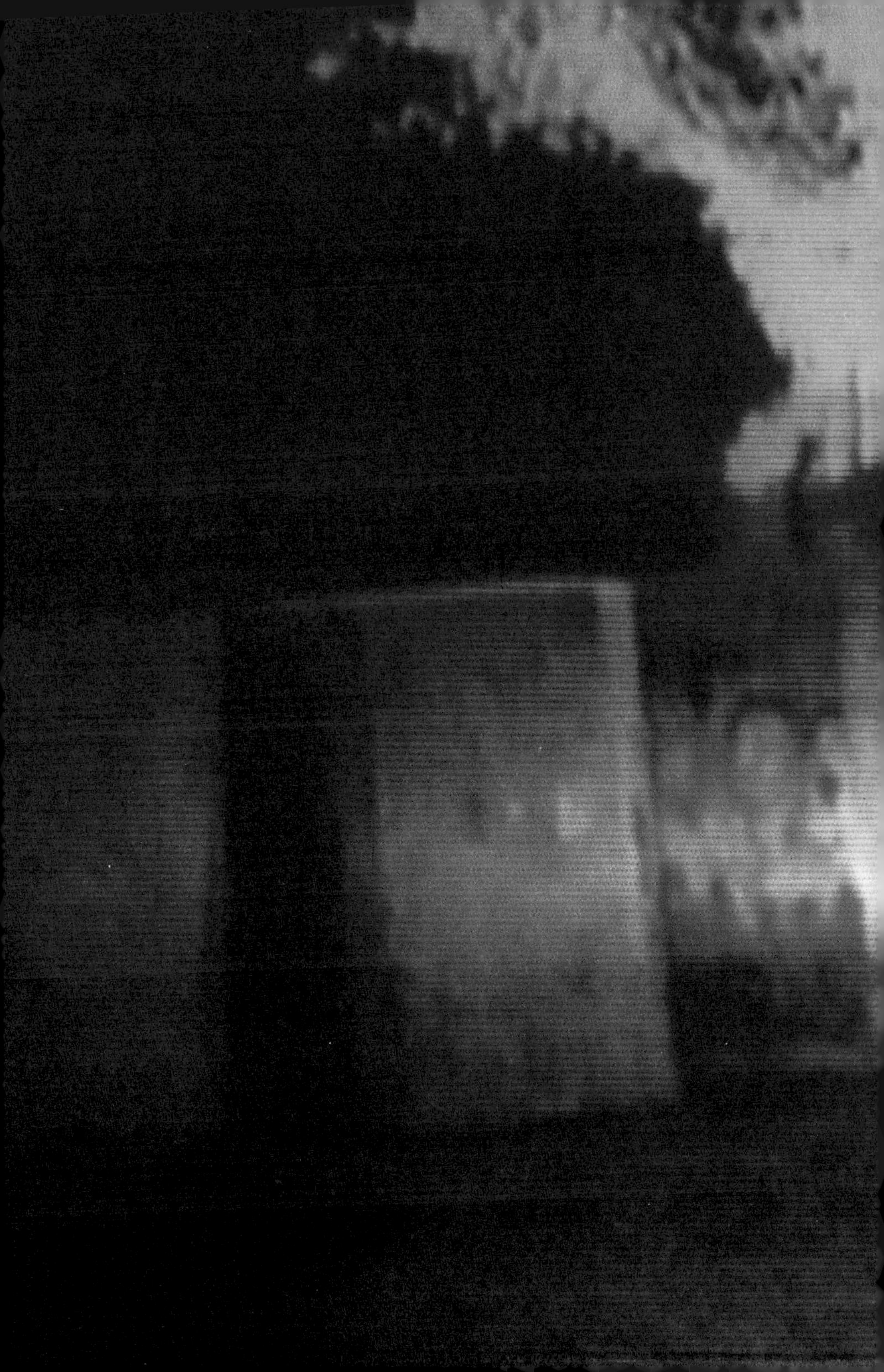

MONA HATOUM |20   21
still from *Measures of Distance*,
1988, pp. 22-23

work's title, the language tired and over-used, eloquent of the
draining of meaning inherent in over-negotiated positions such as
those taken up by the two sides in the Northern Irish conflict over
the many years of its development. At the same time, however, the
phrases work together as found fragments of unintentional poetry,
their tenses looping backwards and forwards across the road ahead
and behind, the work speaking volumes about the expectations and
hopes, frustrations and failures embedded within the Northern Irish
Peace Process and visible at every level, especially in that of the
language used to articulate it.

    Alan Currall's use of the voice-over is somewhat different, although
he, too, plays with ideas of language rendered less than meaningful.
Inspired, as he has said, by 'the tone and manner [...] of the various
shop managers [he has] worked under in [his] career as a shelf-
filler', in his *Word Processing*, 1995 (cat. 11) the artist presents
himself 'explaining' to a microchip the various activities that will be
required of it in the preparation of a simple document. On a video
monitor, we see a microchip – looking rather like a small beetle –
and the finger tips of the artist, tapping to emphasize certain words
as he addresses the chip: 'Right then, now what I want you to do, is,
every time I press down on the keyboard, on one of the letters of
the keyboard, I want you to put that letter up on the screen in front
of me...'. In a parody both of corporate training speak and the kind
of arcane languages we assume computers understand (we all
vaguely know that they speak, or certainly used to in their early
days, something called 'basic', which has something to do with
binary numbers, and is based on simple choices between one option
and another), the instructions get more and more elaborate. The
artist goes through a range of options for 'individual letters and
individual numbers, or groups of letters or groups of numbers' – he
may want them to be bold, 'you know, darker', or italic, 'kind of
slanty', or underlined; or both bold and italic, bold and underlined,
italic and underlined; or even bold and italic and underlined – 'OK?'.
The text is punctuated by the artist's tapping fingers and
unconvincing attempts to ensure the chip is following him, and
ends with every self-taught computer-user's plea: 'Now when that
page comes out of the printer, it's got to be identical to the one on
the screen. That's all I ask'. The artist then withdraws, leaving the
microchip alone on the screen, inscrutable, conveying complete lack
of understanding and leading the viewer to suspect that – just
possibly – the artist has not been speaking quite the right language.

Mona Hatoum's *Measures of Distance*, 1988 (cat. 20) is also a single-screen monitor piece, which uses visual imagery together with both the written and spoken word to create a work that is moving and extremely eloquent about the pain of personal and political separation. The piece opens with the screen filled with hand-written Arabic script, which creates a mesh like barbed-wire, behind which we can just make out someone moving. A soundtrack begins, and we hear two women talking together in Arabic. Then, over the top of this conversation, which continues beneath it, a woman's voice reads out a letter, in English: 'My dear Mona...'. The voice is that of the artist, reading letters from her mother to herself. Throughout the course of the video, five letters are read, each of which begins the same way, with a heartfelt wish that 'this bloody war' would stop so that the writer and recipient could see each other again. Instruments of communication, the letters are clearly an index of separation, their existence dependent solely on the fact that mother and daughter are in different countries.

As the story of the letters unfolds, so does the viewer's understanding of the piece. The images become more distinct, and show a woman – presumably the artist's mother – moving around in the shower. She discusses the imagery in her letters, making reference to the artist's most recent visit, four years previously, when mother and daughter spent time talking and taking photographs, enjoying a new-found intimacy that delighted the mother but, she suspects, shocked the father – 'as if I had given you something that only belongs to him'. The mother's letters respond more and more explicitly to questions contained in the artist's own letters – which we never get to hear – and centre on issues of personal and political identity, as she links the artist's sense of alienation within and without the family to the fact of their exile from Palestine to Lebanon, a move which, she feels, stripped all of them of their identity and sense of pride. Eavesdropping on such a private correspondence, the viewer feels privileged to be part of both women's struggle for understanding, and feels bitterly with them the unfairness of their position. The letters end with the mother explaining that she will be able to write no more, as the post office has been destroyed by a car bomb. She knows it can take days to get a phone connection from London to Beirut, but she begs her daughter to persevere, as this fragile connection is all they have left. Language is itself migratory in this work, moving from conversation to letter to translation, from the spoken to the written word and back again. Its origin in the mind of the individual remains clear, however, as does its power and, on occasion, its powerlessness, to communicate properly the thoughts arising in that mind, and to connect one individual to another.

Mona Hatoum experiments with language, using it as an equivalent to visual imagery, bringing words and images onto the same plane and forcing the viewer to look at and interpret them on the same terms. This is more usually the territory of the non-moving image: over the course of the twentieth century, many artists have invited words into the space of the picture plane, liberating them from their subservient position in a title or caption.

Lisa Milroy shares something of Mona Hatoum's concern that language, while purporting to express thought, may in fact be as much of a barrier to communication as a pathway for it. Her *Doing, Thinking, Speaking*, 2000 (cat. 26) is a large painting of a crowd of people doing things outside on the street. Borrowing from the conventions of cartoons, the artist has given several of the people speech and thought bubbles, which emerge, empty, from their heads. Speech is white and thought is blue, but neither is actually put into words. Perhaps verbal expression is impossible. Perhaps, in fact, it has given way to a different form of expression – that of painting itself. At first glance, the picture looks unfinished. Only one part of the painting is 'properly' worked up. Yet it is finished, and the rhythms that play across its surface are tightly controlled. The sweep of luscious paint in the 'finished' section moves into and on top of the contrasting area of matt, sketched-in outline, advancing and receding with illusionistic depth. This depth is matched by the sumptuous painterliness of the empty blue thought bubbles. As we investigate the picture closely, enjoying its stories, all the present participles of its title begin to refer back to painting – as an activity to be pursued, a mode of thought and a method of speech. The unfinished appearance of the painting adds a past and a potential future to its insistent presents, and it comes to be about the real world and the possibilities for engagement with it as a painter – the use of the habit of painting to explore its potential for communication.

Lisa Milroy brings a marked absence of language into the space of the picture plane. Other artists use language at large in the world outside the image to connect the business of image-making with that of experiencing and thinking about external reality. In the case of Mario Rossi's *The End / Untitled*, 1996-2000 (cat. 30), it is the reality of film that is called upon to inform the image. A series of

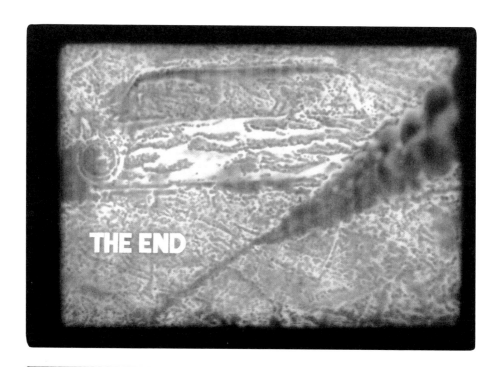

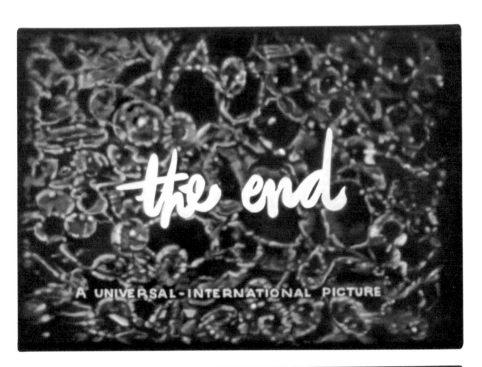

paintings of the words 'The End', all taken from different films, the work draws upon the inclination of words to operate as triggers for past experience. Although the artist does not identify the films from which each particular graphic treatment of 'The End' is taken, some of the paintings are instantly recognizable, the typeface of the two simple words bringing into the space of the picture plane any memories the viewer might have of seeing the film in question.

Gilbert & George's *Smash*, 1977 (cat. 17) and David Hockney's *We Two Boys Together Clinging*, 1961 (cat. 23) both use graffiti, the visual language of the street, to collapse the distinction between art and external reality. Gilbert & George juxtapose photographs of themselves with others of people, places and textures encountered on the streets of London, the whole presided over by the words 'smash', photographed as found. Hockney, on the other hand, seems to absorb the visual style of graffiti into his own painting, producing an image that could almost have been lifted straight from the wall of a public toilet, but that also makes reference to the American poet Walt Whitman, whose poem of the same name begins:

'We two boys together clinging,

One the other never leaving,

Up and down the roads going, North and South excursions making,

Power enjoying, elbows stretching, fingers clutching,

Arm'd and fearless, eating, drinking, sleeping, loving...'.

Hockney uses the first line of the poem as the title of his painting, and as the basis for his mock graffiti. He also writes the fourth and fifth lines at the right hand edge of his image, the words falling out of the picture plane as though they were indeed inscribed on a wall, only a fragment of which the artist, like Gilbert & George perhaps, has reproduced.

Ben Nicholson's incorporation of the word 'boque' into the painting *Boque*, 1932 (cat. 28) is more reminiscent of Cubist use of words and word fragments than of graffiti, making us think of lettering on shop fronts or beer bottles. The word has no meaning in French, although it is clearly intended to be in that language. It may be that Nicholson wanted it to be read more as pattern than as a word whose meaning could and should be deciphered, as many of his paintings of the period play with spatial illusion and recession into depth while remaining faithful to the reality of the picture plane. Writing on the canvas is one way of insisting upon the reality of a painting as canvas, of bringing the space in a picture right up close to its surface.

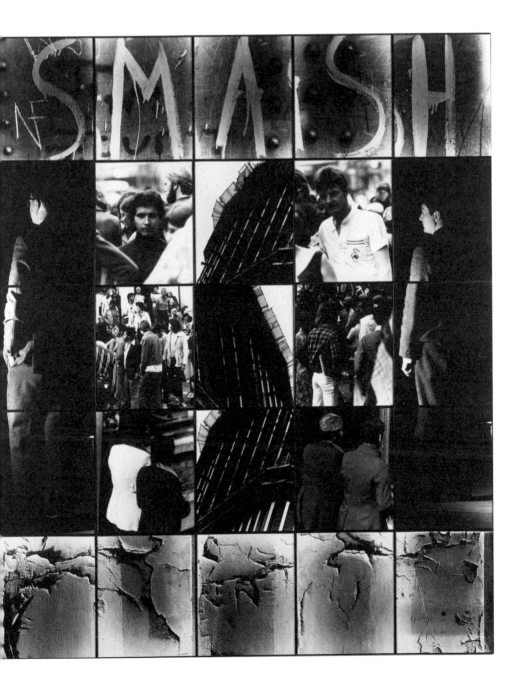

Nicholson's use of the word 'boque', and Hockney and Gilbert & George's appropriation of the found languages of the street are strongly reminiscent of the way language operates in Cubism and Surrealism. Cubist artists began incorporating words and word fragments into their work initially in the form of collage, using newsprint and labels from wine and beer bottles literally to bring the external world into the realm of the pictorial. Later, they began to mimic the typographical styles of newspaper headlines or other lettering found in the bar or the café, painting words onto the picture plane to add further complexity to the spatial games played by their painted realities.

Surrealism was as much about writing as it was about painting and sculpture. The first members of the movement were poets, and much of their research into the operation of the unconscious mind and the way in which it might influence and in turn be influenced by the creative arts was carried out at a level of language: 'there is no thought outside of language. All Surrealism supports this proposition' (Louis Aragon). Agreeing with Sigmund Freud that language operates as a trigger for the unconscious, revealing long-buried thoughts, Surrealist artists often used words alongside visual imagery, confident that they would contribute to the movement's aim to propel the viewer into a state of the 'marvelous'; a state of heightened awareness akin to dreaming, in which an individual is fully alive to the potential of his or her unconscious mind. The language the Surrealists used drew on a number of sources. They looked to their own poetry, or the poetry of previous writers they admired (chief among these being the Comte de Lautréamont, author of the phrase the Surrealists adopted almost as a mantra – 'as beautiful as the chance encounter of an umbrella and a sewing machine on a dissecting table'). They were interested in what they termed 'automatic' language – language generated spontaneously, spoken aloud or written down without any pre-conceived idea as to what might be produced. They were also passionate collectors of striking word fragments, words and phrases encountered on the street, the attention they paid to them part of a deliberate strategy of remaining open to what they termed 'objective chance'.

Simon Linke is a contemporary artist who works on the boundary between conscious and unconscious thought and action. His *Lost*, 1996 (cat. 25) is a painting of a simple sentence. The words are treated as interesting graphic marks in themselves, but also form a sentence implying a narrative ('I found the car keys on the

I found the car keys on the marmalade lid in the fridge.

RENTS TO BE PAID AT POST OFFICES?

CPRE says gravel plan is too enormous

PSYCHIATRIC DAY HOSPITAL IN TOWN?

COMPLAIN GAS MEN CALL BUT GO TOO SOON

Box and tools stolen

WILL COUNCIL GO FOR CLUB AS CENTRE?

7

Protective netting now is in need of repair

Quartet tuned-in for a busy year

TOO MUCH SHARING OF CAR PARK IS NOT RECOMMENDED	'Demand for houses with outstrip supply'	AFTER HOLIDAY RE-OPENING OF SWIMMING POOL DELAYED

DAY CLOSURE OF BY-PASS FOR REPAIRS

VILLAGES FOUND THAT ROAD-GRITTING VARIED

Woman hurt in fall from cycle | Shelter damaged

MORE PLANNING APPLICATIONS

FIRM PLANS TO BUILD AN EXTENSION TO ITS FACTORY

BOUNDARY COMPROMISE

Fluoride or not? parish meeting to decide

'RIDICULOUS' FELLING OF THE TREES

IT OWNS CENTRE SITE!

Formation of theatre club

SOME BINS NOT EMPTIED FOR 3 WEEKS

MANY PIPE BURSTS WHILE TENANTS AWAY

EXPLANATION ABOUT PLAN PERMIT DELAY

That's what a battery is for!

Asking only for replacement of road markings

Reluctant at first to add one more member, council welcomed idea

COULD REVERT TO ITS FORMER USE

Scrap car found in river

A POPULAR SECTION!

Appointed new manager

Omission of part of path near stream would be 'unacceptable loss'

Butcher plans to make extension to shop premises

Pantomime-type of Nativity story

Smashed by snowball

POLICY ON REPAIRS IS EXPLAINED

WIDESPREAD EFFECTS ARE BEING FELT

NO CASH FOR ALTERATIONS

A malicious call

VANDALISM IN CEMETERY

'Business as usual' in the new premises

Window smashed

Adults school is entertained

ACTION GROUP TO SHOW COUNCILLORS?

TWO LAMPS TO BRIGHTEN LANE

NEW SIGN WOULD BE OUT OF CHARACTER

Put out rubbish fire

Chimney fire

JOINS IN A PARTNERSHIP

IS GETTING BETTER

Business as usual at swimming pool

Passed on requ

Five sewage pumping stations put out of action due to floods

Only a little trouble

FAILED TO MAKE MOST OF CHANCES

WONDERED WHY NO ACTION WAS TAKEN

COMPROMISE IS REACHED

WAR EMERGENCY EXERCISE

MORE BIBLES

LIBRARY FIGURES FLUCTUATE

To consider action to improve property

ROLLER DAMAGE TO FENCE PRODUCES SOME COMMENTS

WATER NO LONGER RAN OFF PAVEMENT

WARNS, DIFFICULTIES COULD GET WORSE

Theft from a shed

Man's sudden death

CALL FOR HOME SAFETY SCHEMES

ASH PROBLEMS COUNCILLORS ARE TO ACT

Industrialists join in festival displays

He gave guests a personal welcome

Chimney fire

Church clock just back in chime

Rider injured when motor-cycle skids

Cannot now stand

Be warm – but be safe too!

ADMITS DAMAGING A CAR WINDOW

Vandals cause £275 damage to car tyres

LOOKING FOR TREES TO BE PRESERVED

MOUNTAIN MAN IS SPEAKER

Theft of cash box House extension

Theft of equipment

To Japan and Honolulu

Clearance of waterways

President also models hair style

OLD SEWERAGE SYSTEM STARTING TO CRACK UP

Asks about its right to an open space

ILL WIND DOES GOOD

Radio stolen from bag

His hobby, to give colour to stations

Executive will still have a seat

'Stupid' offence after too much drink

CAR STOPPED NEAR A 10-FOOT DROP

AFTER BREAK-IN THIEV RETURN TO APOLOGISE

CYCLIST PUSHING A CYCLE IS NOT A PEDESTRIAN

Cash and disco tickets stolen

A DARING COMEDY FARCE

A secondary floodbank or rubble

Officers feel bowls centre inappropriate to the area

A DRAMATIC CHANGE IN PART OF TOWN

SOME EX-SERVICEMEN ARE NOW POLICE OFFICERS

Bitter weather thwarted speaker

'left over'?

AREA HEALTH AUTHORITY INTERESTED

HIS AIM IS TO MAKE YOU SMILE

APPROVAL FOR PLAN

Community hall? survey to be made of club

Firm feels penalised and offers tour of works

The elusive state of happiness

Favourable response

BOROUGH RATE COULD STAY UNCHANGED

Yes to plan for premises empty for four years

TO TAKE ANOTHER LOOK AT PLAN

to proposed relief road petition

PLAN FOR COLD STOR IN STREET OFF BUSY ROAD IS TURNED DOW

Motorist's fine offences

Feeler for school

Want council to reconsider amusements centre plan

marmalade lid in the fridge') and a particularly distracted mental state. Ian Breakwell's *The Elusive State of Happiness*, 1979 (cat. 9), a collage consisting of a photo-booth portrait of an unknown man and headlines culled from local newspapers, has something of the unintentional poetry of objective chance – as viewers, we must read into the headlines what we can.

Perhaps the best known Surrealist user of language was René Magritte, whose axiomatic 'ceci n'est pas une pipe' (this is not a pipe), set against the image of a pipe, has become one of the touchstones of Surrealism. Magritte worked with language as one code among many, making it clear that the connection between words and the objects they describe is nothing more than convention – 'this' (whether the word pipe or a picture of a pipe) is not, clearly, a pipe.

The notion of language as a code or convention is one that has been tremendously influential on contemporary art. Words can replace imagery completely, operating in the place of absent imagery or experience. Hamish Fulton uses language as a trigger both for his own memories and the viewer's imagination. His work takes the form of walks, which he documents, not only through photographs, but also in words. Presented in the gallery as objects to be looked at, the words he chooses to describe his walks become loaded with significance, summoning myriad possibilities in the mind's eye – 'seven winds seven twigs seven paths, seven days walking and seven nights camping in a wood Scotland March 1985' (cat. 14).

S E V E N

W I N D S

S E V E N

T W I G S

S E V E N

P A T H S

SEVEN DAYS WALKING AND SEVEN NIGHTS CAMPING IN A WOOD SCOTLAND MARCH 1985

HAMISH FULTON |15
Untitled, Japan 1986, from
Fourteen Works, 1982-89

金 ROCK
土 EARTH
日 SUN
月 MOON
火 FIRE
水 WATER
木 WOOD
金 ROCK

土 EARTH
日 SUN
月 MOON
火 FIRE
水 WATER
木 WOOD
金 ROCK
土 EARTH

A SIXTEEN DAY WALKING JOURNEY FROM THE SHIP AT NACHI KATSUURA TO THE TRAIN AT HORYUJI
TRAVELLING BY WAY OF NARA JAPAN EARLY 1986

Douglas Gordon's *Painting No 19: Mark Rothko / Betty Parsons*, 1992 (cat. 18) also uses language to replace experience – this time the experience of looking at art. Again, the artist is using language as a coded reference, but now to the rather more closed world of recent art history. As viewers, we need more information, a key of some kind, to crack this code. A clue is provided by the painterly qualities of the picture's background, which are in fact standing in for another painting's foreground. The picture consists of the words 'Korea Goes to War' and the date 1951, painted on a monochromatic background. The work plays a game with the viewer, the words making a specific reference to a particular painting by the American Abstract Expressionist painter Mark Rothko, entitled *Korea Goes to War*, 1951, exhibited at the Betty Parsons Gallery in New York.

Simon Patterson's *The Great Bear*, 1992 (cat. 29) could be seen as operating similarly, as a kind of 'in joke' for the initiated. The artist reproduces the London Underground Map. Many of us will have a residual knowledge of the map lurking in the back of our minds and ready to spring to the forefront as summoned by the artist. Instead of replacing one kind of code with another – words for a walk, for example – Patterson remains faithful to the kind of code operating within the map as it usually is, changing its key, so that in our imagination we can travel down lines and through stations named after engineers, explorers, footballers or musicians rather than the more prosaic geographical and historical markers to which we are more accustomed. Who would not prefer to get out of the tube at Gina Lollobrigida than at Tottenham Court Road?

Korea
Goes To
War

1951

The Great Bear

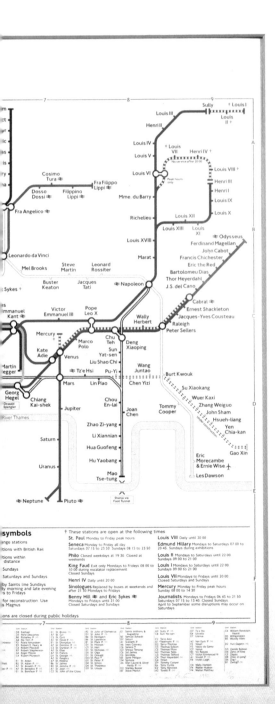

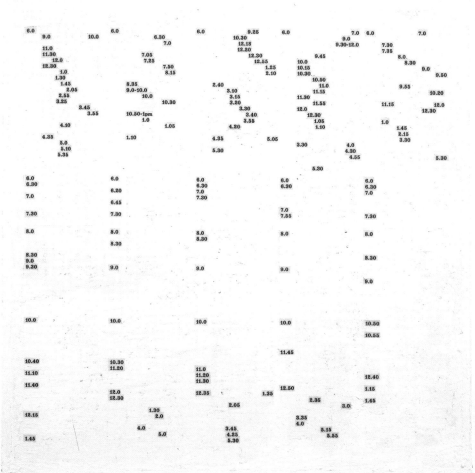

Tony Morgan's *Le Mot*, 1993 (cat. 27) takes us back to Magritte's
pipe, his painting of the word 'word', in French, spinning a web of
complication around a simple rendering of an object – but can a
word be an object? Louise Hopkins and Alan Ball perhaps think so,
as both artists physically erase rather than replace the coded
languages with which they work. Ball uses a television schedule as a
rubric for a particular day, and paints on it with correction fluid,
removing one pattern (that of the words) in order to create another,
or series of others; in his words 'a supermarket receipt [...] the
punched scroll of an old pre-programmed piano [...] the sequency
gel of human DNA [...] the dynamics of viewing [...] the remains of
the day'. Hopkins also works with erasure, although in her case it is
a matter always of finding an appropriate mark with which to
counter the marks on the surface with which she starts. In
Songsheet 4, 1996 (cat. 24) the mark she finds is the exact equivalent
of the marks of the song-sheet to the popular song by Don Gibson,
'I Can't Stop Loving You', and the work consists in the complete
undoing – or re-doing in white instead of black – of the
transcription of the song into printed words and musical notation.
The artist has commented, 'It is as if a potential already present in
the object is re-used or fine tuned in some way to change the
framework through which it is viewed'.

Ian Hamilton Finlay is less interested in language as a code, preferring instead to respond to its potential for metaphoric and aesthetic richness. An artist who is well known for works that take the form of concrete poems or artist's books, his *Strawberry Camouflage*, 1977 (cat. 19) is part of a group of neon poems he made in the 1970s. A title which is a complete poem in itself, the piece operates with an extreme economy of means which nevertheless results in an intense and extravagant beauty. Both the colour and the typographical arrangement of the neon letters are suggested by the meaning of the words they shape, so that the work resonates with a satisfying circularity, signaling first within itself, then appealing to the aesthetic sensibility and linguistic comprehension of the viewer.

Strawberry Camouflage, 1977

Some coded systems are embedded so deeply into the social and
cultural fabric of contemporary life that artists may make reference
to them, secure in the knowledge that the meaning they collect
around them in their more familiar context will continue to cling to
them even as they are subverted for use in the gallery. Martin Boyce
and Ross Sinclair use the political slogan, appropriating both the
kinds of words used in slogans, and the supports on which we often
find these words. Boyce is interested in the specificity of the
language he uses in his mock placards (cat. 8). Compiling a list of
old slogans, some universal, some specific to particularly British
issues, the artist noted that 'some were redundant because the cause
had been won or lost, but with others it was the language that was
redundant. Those words in that configuration were simply
unfashionable. We couldn't say them even if we had to'. Sinclair's
T-shirts (cat. 33) seem similarly absurd. Part of a series the artist has
been making since 1993, hand-painting T-shirts with song titles,
puns on crass, pseudo-American slogans, phrases taken from
literature and philosophy and snippets from conversations overheard
in pubs, the T-shirts take their cue from the urgent political
statements worn on T-shirts since the 1960s, a trend culminating in
Britain at least in Katherine Hamnett's famous meeting with Prime
Minister Margaret Thatcher at which she wore a T-shirt proclaiming
'70% don't want Pershing'. In the hands of Sinclair, passionate
political commitment is undermined by the popular culture he
quotes, and the T-shirt is relegated to the realm of banal souvenir
('my mate went to London and all I got was this lousy T-shirt...',
etc) rather than the vehicle for radical change it may once, in
context, have been considered.

MARTIN BOYCE |8
*Souvenir Placards (Standard
Edition)*, 1993

ROSS SINCLAIR |33
T-Shirt Paintings, 1993-98,
pp. 54-55

53

ONLY 9.99

TEARS ARE COOL

NAG NAG NAG

I WAS BORN DEAD

CALIFORNIA UBER ALLES

OST YED

KNOLL GALERIE WIEN 93/94

SIXTY 69 NINE

KED HE DAY WERE RN

PERVERT £

HA TE

AR IS VER YOU NT IT

I NEED MORE

CONSPIRAC THEORIS

Tracey Emin's *The Simple Truth*, 1995 (cat. 13) also reads like some kind of pseudo-slogan: 'Tracey Emin: here to stay'. In conversation, however, the artist has revealed the work to be something of a personal manifesto. The piece was made during an extended visit to the United States, which was not going according to plan. Rather than an artwork, the artist made it simply as a bedspread for the bed in her hotel room, intending to cheer herself up and to remind herself of her commitment to herself and her art: 'I made this blanket in response to my feelings about America and also to the art world. It was never a work intended to sell – or to be hung – but to be placed on my bed in my hotel room. This is why it is so simple in comparison to my other sewn works. I could have quite easily sewn the words FUCK YOU ALL or I'LL BE BACK – but instead I made a positive response – TRACY EMIN HERE TO STAY – basically, whether people want it or not'.

In this, as in many works that consist of words instead of images, rather than words as well as images, the choice of words and the form used to convey them assume equal importance. Keith Arnatt writes his *Is it Possible for me to do Nothing as my Contribution to this Exhibition?*, 1970 (cat. 1) as a typed proposal, the kind of artist's statement one might expect to receive from an artist in response to an invitation to participate in an exhibition, or perhaps one that might be intended to be displayed as an information label alongside an artwork. The proposal is, however, the artwork itself, the artist moving from future to past tense in the course of an involved discourse on the nature of nothingness and the meaning of the word nothing.

TRACEY EMIN |13
The Simple Truth, 1995

KEITH ARNATT |1
*Is it Possible for me to do
Nothing as my Contribution to this
Exhibition?*, 1970, pp. 58-59

57

IS IT POSSIBLE FOR ME TO DO NOTHING AS
MY CONTRIBUTION TO THIS EXHIBITION?

To put forward the notion THAT I HAVE DONE NOTHING as my contribution
to this exhibition might appear to be slightly unreasonable. Moreover, a
request to 'utilise' a certain amount of gallery space during the course of
the exhibition in which 'to do nothing', seems to compound this unreasonable-
ness. Nevertheless, in putting forward such a notion and making such a
request it becomes necessary to consider some of the questions that could
be asked of such a 'contribution'.

The questions that come immediately to mind are (a), Am I simply putting
forward an IDEA as my contribution to the exhibition, that is, the idea that
I have done nothing? Or (b), Am I putting forward a CLAIM as my
contribution to the exhibition, i.e., the claim that I have done nothing?
These questions, in turn, raise the further (ontological) question which
has to do with the 'substance' of my contribution. If, for instance, my
contribution to this exhibition is taken to be an IDEA or a CLAIM, one
might wish to know, exactly, what the respective modes of existence of
the IDEA or the CLAIM in question are. However, there is perhaps no
need to answer this particular question here, for the view I have of what
I call "my contribution to this exhibition" is that it is neither just the IDEA
or just the CLAIM. It is, rather, a STATE OF AFFAIRS arising from (I),
My being invited to contribute to this exhibition, and (2), My acceptance
of the invitation to contribute to this exhibition, and finally (3), My
condition of acceptance of the invitation to contribute to this exhibition
is that I DO NOTHING as my 'contribution'. It is, then, the EVIDENCE
(or perhaps we should say - the lack of it) in support of my claim to have
done nothing as my contribution to this exhibition which is the 'substance'
of my contribution to this exhibition.

The expression "I have done nothing" has, of course, no literal meaning:
it's meaning (or sense) will depend upon the context in which it is used.
In the context of this exhibition how, then, might the use of this expression
be understood? It might be taken to mean that I have done no 'work' of
which there is evidence (of one kind or another) in the exhibition. But
such an interpretation would have to exclude the means whereby the idea
that I have done nothing as my contribution to this exhibition is communicated
in the first place. This written material, itself, is evidence of having done
something.

The absence of this written information (or its spoken equivalent) would, of course, raise the question "How could it be known that I have done nothing as my contribution to this exhibition?" If my name only appeared in the exhibition catalogue, a reader would assume that I was participating in the exhibition by contributing a 'work' or 'works'. On seeing no such evidence of work - either in the gallery or in the catalogue - it is unlikely that he would regard my NAME (printed in the catalogue) as a contribution to the exhibition. He is more likely, I think, to assume that I had not contributed to the exhibition - that I had omitted to do so. But perhaps this understandable reaction, on his part, is parasitic upon his assumption that my 'contribution' would take a more 'conventional' form or deal with a more 'orthodox' subject-matter.

One might consider the question "Is it possible for me to do nothing as my contribution to this exhibition?" in a quite different light however. The expression "I have done nothing", or "He has done nothing", might be used (quite colloquially) to mean I HAVE DONE NOTHING SIGNIFICANT, that is, it might be used to express the belief that my 'contribution' is in no way important or significant. What criteria, of course, one wishes to invoke for the 'significance' of a contribution to an art-exhibition is another matter. But, looking at the originally posed question in this particular light, I admit that it is at least possible that I have contributed NOTHING to this exhibition. And some, I have no doubt, would say that this is, indeed, the case.

KEITH ARNATT 1970

Anya Gallaccio, working twenty-five years later but operating within a similar system, makes an intensely beautiful object out of her instruction piece *'Place a Candle'*, 1996 (cat. 16). Pure potential, the piece consists of an etched glass plate, bearing the instructions to light a candle, place it on the glass and let it burn. Both of these works shift theoretical power from artist to viewer and back again: it is up to us to decide if Arnatt's proposition is acceptable as art, or whether we are prepared imaginatively to comply with Gallaccio's instructions and complete the sculpture she has begun.

Fiona Banner's *The desert*, 1994-95 (cat. 5) is already elaborately, insistently complete. A transcription, in the artist's own words, of the events of the film *Lawrence of Arabia*, it unfurls across a huge length of gallery wall. All artworks need to be read, but this insists upon the process more than most – the viewer has physically to walk the length of the work, attempting to keep the meaning of the words together as they threaten to move out of line. Time becomes an intrinsic part of the work – it is a record of the duration of a film, but also a diary of a portion of the artist's life. If we choose to engage fully with it, it becomes a representation of the time we too have spent.

Writing and reading, no less than painting and looking, are demanding, time-based activities. More familiar to most of us than the more habitual activities of the artist, they enlist a particular complicity – we feel, perhaps, more able to join in. The capacity of words to encourage active participation and understanding on the part of the viewer is one of the reasons for their use throughout twentieth and twenty-first centuries. Language is a common medium – if you can speak the right words, you may find a direct way into another person's brain. If this can be true of 'real' language, it may also be true of nonsense or involuntary language, the kind of automatic language that so intrigued the Surrealists. For them, the form taken by such words was again almost as important as their content, and often led into drawing and painting. Susan Hiller's *Midnight, Baker Street*, 1983 (cat. 21) plays around with several of these ideas: over images of herself taken in an automatic photo booth at night, she doodles and scribbles. The implication that she may be accessing some kind of hidden truth about her inner psyche is irresistible: which tells us more about her, the image taken by a machine, its impersonality guaranteeing its impartiality, or the 'language' rising unbidden from her brain?

Words and the form of words run throughout all the works in this book. Yet they are immensely varied, from dry text pieces to beautiful, sensuous neon; from austere rendering of single sentences to elaborate video soundtracks. Artists' engagement with language as a visual and conceptual tool takes many forms, and offers a number of ways to explore the potential of a means of communication we may too often take for granted.

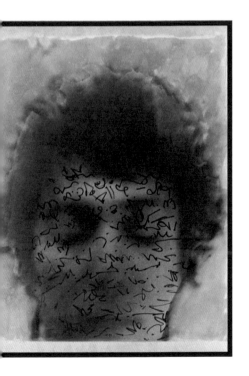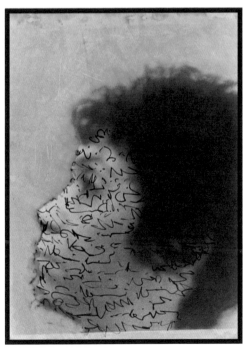

LIST OF WORKS

1 (pp. 58-59)
KEITH ARNATT
Is it Possible for me to do Nothing as my Contribution to this Exhibition?, 1970
text
76.2 x 101.6 cm
purchased 1973

2
ALAN BALL
Untitled (Sat, 29/01/00), 2000
newspaper and correction fluid on canvas
25.5 x 25.5 cm
purchased 2000

3 (p. 44)
ALAN BALL
Untitled (Mon, 7/02/00), 2000
newspaper and correction fluid on canvas
25.5 x 25.5 cm
purchased 2000

4
ALAN BALL
Untitled (Wed, 23/02/00), 2000
newspaper and correction fluid on canvas
25.5 x 25.5 cm
purchased 2000

5 (pp. 62-63)
FIONA BANNER
The desert, 1994-95
silkscreen print (in 6 parts)
235 x 518.5 cm
purchased 2001
Photograph courtesy of Frith Street Gallery, London

6 (p. 10)
GLEN BAXTER
"I find his attempts to clarify the neo-plasticist stance a trifle wearing" muttered Ken, 1978
ink on paper
40.6 x 29.1 cm
purchased 1979

7 (p. 11)
GLEN BAXTER
"To me the window is still a symbolically loaded motif" drawled Cody, 1981
ink on paper
39.1 x 25.9 cm
purchased 1981

8 (p. 53)
MARTIN BOYCE
Souvenir Placards (Standard Edition), 1993
plywood, wood, emulsion paint and gloss paint
7 placards, dimensions variable
Gift of Charles Saatchi, 1999

9 (p. 36)
IAN BREAKWELL
The Elusive State of Happiness, 1979
collage (newsprint and photograph mounted on board)
59 x 46 cm
purchased 2000

10 (pp. 14-15)
MICHAEL CRAIG-MARTIN
Kid's Stuff 1-7, 1973
mirror, tape and text on plastic (seven pieces)
40.6 x 30.5 cm each
purchased 1974

11 (p. 20)
ALAN CURRALL
Word Processing, 1995
single screen video (monitor)
running time: 6 minutes
purchased 1997

12 (pp. 18-19)
WILLIE DOHERTY
At the End of the Day, 1994
video projection
running time: 30 minutes
purchased 1995
Photograph by Mimmo Capone, Courtesy of Matt's Gallery, London

13 (p. 57)
TRACEY EMIN
The Simple Truth, 1995
wool and cotton
216 x 235 cm
purchased 1998
Photograph: Stephen White

14 (p. 38)
HAMISH FULTON
Seven Winds, Scotland 1985, from *Fourteen Works*, 1982-89
offset lithograph
107 x 83 cm
edition 30 of 35
purchased 1993
© The Paragon Press and Hamish Fulton

15 (p. 39)
HAMISH FULTON
Untitled, Japan 1986, from *Fourteen Works*, 1982-89
offset lithograph
98 x 69 cm
purchased 1993
© The Paragon Press and Hamish Fulton

16 (p. 61)
ANYA GALLACCIO
'Place a Candle', 1996
glass, wood, wax and cotton
50 x 50 x 5 cm
purchased 1996

17 (p. 31)
GILBERT & GEORGE
Smash, 1977
photo-piece (25 panels)
302.5 x 252.5 cm
purchased 1981

18 (p. 41)
DOUGLAS GORDON
Painting No. 19: Mark Rothko / Betty Parsons, 1992
acrylic on canvas
100 x 66 cm
purchased 1992

19 (pp. 50-51)
IAN HAMILTON FINLAY
Strawberry Camouflage, 1977
neon, board, wood and metal
40.8 x 137 x 12.5 cm
purchased 1977

20 (pp. 22-23)
MONA HATOUM
Measures of Distance, 1988
single screen video (monitor)
running time: 15 minutes, 26 seconds
purchased 1999

21 (pp. 64-65)
SUSAN HILLER
Midnight, Baker Street, 1983
c-type photographs on Agfa Lustre paper 3-1/2, on 3 panels
71 x 51 cm each
purchased 1984

22 (p. 17)
JOHN HILLIARD
Cause of Death, 1974
black and white photographs and
text on card, 4 sections
28.5 x 14.5 cm each
purchased 1974

23 (p. 32)
DAVID HOCKNEY
We Two Boys Together Clinging,
1961
oil on board
121.9 x 152.4 cm
purchased 1961
© David Hockney
Photograph: John Webb

24 (pp. 46-47)
LOUISE HOPKINS
Songsheet 4, 1996
acrylic ink on songsheet of
love song
30.4 x 45.7 cm
purchased 1997

25 (p. 35)
SIMON LINKE
Lost, 1996
oil on canvas
126.9 x 89.6 cm
purchased 1997

26 (pp. 26-27)
LISA MILROY
Doing, Thinking, Speaking, 2000
oil and acrylic on canvas
193 x 305.5 cm
purchased 2001
© Lisa Milroy 2002

27 (pp. 48-49)
TONY MORGAN
Le Mot, 1993
oil and acrylic on canvas
72 cm x 24.5 cm
purchased 2000

28 (pp. 33)
BEN NICHOLSON
Bocque, 1932
oil on board
48 x 78.5 cm
purchased 1950
© Angela Verren-Taunt 2002

29 (pp. 42-43)
SIMON PATTERSON
The Great Bear, 1992
4-colour lithograph on paper
with anodized aluminium
99 x 124.4 cm
edition 25 of 50
purchased 1993
© Simon Patterson and
Transport for London 2002
Photograph: John Webb

30 (pp. 28-29)
MARIO ROSSI
The End / Untitled, 1996-2000
acrylic on canvas (5 parts from
a series)
61 x 86.5 cm each
purchased 2001

31 (p. 13)
DAVID SHRIGLEY
*'See the little creature in the giant
cage...'*, 1998
marker ink on paper
24 x 21 cm
purchased 1999

32
DAVID SHRIGLEY
'The road to beasthood...', 1998
marker ink on paper
24 x 20.5 cm
purchased 1999

33 (pp. 54-55)
ROSS SINCLAIR
T-Shirt Paintings, 1993-98
gesso and acrylic on cotton
(80 from a series)
61 x 61 cm each
purchased 1999

All works belong to the Arts
Council Collection

"Ali," he puts his hands on his hips "... does your father still steal?" Ali stands bolt upright, "No, does Auda

oday?..." He jumps to the ground and adds sarcastically "... Howeitat hospitality?" Auda turns round and po

are that you dine with me at my camp!" A colossal rock looms out of the desert. It dwarfs everything around

at the camp galloping in a group. The scene's frantic, everything is only partially visible through the hazy d

. As for me I cannot serve." Lawrence looks up and says in an accusatory tone, "You commit the Turks to s

en proudly, "I carry twenty-five great wounds, all got in battle... Seventy five men have I killed with my ow

they pay me, and you will tell me if this is a servant's wages!" He glances across the crowd, "... They pay m

bitterly to himself, "My mother mated with a Scorpion!" The picture slowly dissolves into bright daylight. A

rds it gets louder and louder. Lawrence looks across at the massive rocks which flank their path and sees alr

hing out beyond it. Turning to Lawrence, his voice filled with longing, he sighs in disbelief, "Yes... Aqaba!"

es him. Another commotion is occurring nearby, again men seem to be crowding around someone. A man is

must die." "Hummm." "If he dies will it content the Howeitat?" There is a long silence, before Auda answer

asim is breathing heavily now, panting, trembling before Lawrence's gun. He nods his head. Lawrence brac

and shock. He holds out at his hand and looks at the gun. As he looks down at his hand his face is masked w

storming army as they career round the corner. As he fires, a tremendous boom resounds over the noise of h

all headfirst into the sand and toss their riders off in front of them. Another horse flies across the foreground

waves have wet the sand, so that it reflects the sunset. The camel's rider is visible, close up. Then the desert is

foreground. Auda comes from behind it wielding a huge stick. It crashes into some furniture which splinters

e Generals we have taken Aqaba, the Generals would laugh." "I see... " He sounds contemptuous. "In Cairo

come to Aqaba for gold?" Auda descends further, "I came for pleasure as you said... but gold is honourable

eyes narrow on the diminishing figure of Lawrence, his expression doesn't change, but it dissolves, the light

st the horizon. Gradually the rocks turn to mountains which flank a huge flat area of desert. Ahead the dead s

of the wind dims and the storm passes across them into the distance. Sunlight shafts down onto them. Lawre

he of the boys take the lead. Daoud appears, a dark silhouette, at the top of a massive sand dune in the backg

now. He gives a desperate scream, hands around his mouth, "Lawrence...!" His cry can just be heard over th

d. Lawrence tugs off his head scarf, unravels it and flings it across to Daoud. Daoud's moaning uselessly. He

til it is only a small depression. there is nothing else, only the desert. Lawrence and Ramesh emerge from a

place come into view. Uprights and glass-less window frames pass in the foreground. A rusty hinge can be

at him. The dried dirt on his face darkens like mud. He seems to come awake, and looks over at Ramish, sa

l. The bright blue sky frames them from their waists upwards. The sun glares orange on their dusty faces. T

he faint ring of a bell gets louder and louder, a crowded bus streaks across the foreground - a seamless blur

Their footsteps echo on the marble floor. They walk through to another room, its entrance flanked with two

A group of men smoking and playing snooker stop to stare at them as they head straight over to the bar. By

to get rid of you anyway!" Lawrence turns on him and grabs his arm, and stares at him very intensely. The s

of them, too many really... We'll manage it better next time!" As he finishes his sentence, he gulps the lemo

yes of course!" Lawrence realises Brighton thinks it's for him. He's furious as he says, pointing a straight ar

hing in Lawrence's mind. He stares back at Brighton, not leaving his gaze until he sees that the smile has di

's no doubt about it!" Suddenly his tone changes from quite pleasant to extremely accusatory, he almost yell

ened El Arish and Gaza." The General shifts his weight further forwards and asks, "Is there anything else?"

by barks back, "Why not!" It's hard to hear Lawrences answer, "Well, errr... mmm... let me see, sir... I killed

ys facetiously, "Oh yes... entirely!" The General walks over to Lawrence, and pointing at his head demands,

ment, then adds with an emotional quake to his voice, "It was a brilliant bit of soldiering!" Lawrence stares a

ou know of better?" Two soldiers are walking up the stairs. They see the General and Lawrence coming tow

t thigh, pushing himself upright. He looks at the General. His voice is passionate, "A thousand Arabs means

Arabia's for the Arabs now!" His eyes look from left to right, taking in the expressions of each of the men. D

no ambitions in Arabia." The General plonks down his beer glass, pauses a little and declares, "Certainly!"

en?" Dryden answers, "It can be done, sir." Lawrence carries on as if he's speaking a mental list, "... a coup

cked room, then realises that he's surrounded. He turns slowly around but there's no way out behind. There'

atic, yet matter of fact. "Then I can't give them artillery!" "That's for you to say sir." "No, it's not. I've got c

The old man answers him plainly, "No." The American continues, "You know him though?" The old man s

rs, "Not altogether, sir, no." Faisel leans forwards a little and answers him. "Well Mr. Bentley, you will find

rd correctly "Excuse me?" Bentley explains, "... A clever man." Faisal repeats, amused, "Slim customer... v

a?" Faisal answers him, "Oh yes. In this country Mr Bentley, the man who gives victory in battle is prized be

s across at Bentley "Why should you suppose so?" "Well it's just that I heard in Cairo that Major Lawrence

en sent to find material which will show our people that this war is..." Faisal interrupts, "Enjoyable?" Bentl

ing. Bentley frantically snaps away. They feed bullets through a machine gun maniacally. Then Bentley jun

air. They pelt over to the tracks, kicking up sand behind them. They smash